My HOLY HOUR
St. Padre Pio

A Devotional Journal

Season: _____

Date: _____

Belongs to: _____

My Holy Hour - St. Padre Pio is part of the *My Holy Hour Devotional Journal Series.* While all journals will have some similar structure and intent, each one will have minor changes to make it unique. Cover image depicts *St. Padre Pio.*

Go to our website for a free copy of
How to Use a Prayer Journal during Holy Hour
www.HolyHourBooks.com

Holy Hour Books
P.O. Box 430577
Houston, TX 77243

My Holy Hour Devotional Journals

ISBN-13: 978-1-941303-79-5
ISBN-10: 1-941303-79-X

First Printing: 2018

Holy Hour Books is an imprint of Ordinary Matters Publishing.

Printed in the United States of America

*"Jesus, truly present in the Most Blessed Sacrament,
I love You above all things
and I desire to possess You within my soul.
Since I am unable at this moment
to receive You sacramentally,
come at least spiritually into my heart.
I embrace You as being already there,
and unite myself wholly to You.
Never permit me to be separated from You. Amen."*

— *Spiritual Communion Prayer said throughout the day by
St. Padre Pio*

Why Keep a Holy Hour

"First, the Holy Hour is not a devotion; it is a sharing in the work of redemption... our Lord asked: 'Could you not watch one hour with Me?'. In other words, he asked for an hour of reparation to combat the hour of evil; an hour of victimal union with the Cross to overcome the anti-love of sin.

Secondly, the only time Our Lord asked the Apostles for anything was the night he went into his agony... As often in the history of the Church since that time, evil was awake, but the disciples were asleep. That is why there came out of His anguished and lonely Heart the sigh: 'Could you not watch one hour with me?' Not for an hour of activity did He plead, but for an hour of companionship.

The third reason I keep up the Holy Hour is to grow more and more into his likeness. As Paul puts it: "We are transfigured into his likeness, from splendor to splendor.' We become like that which we gaze upon. Looking into a sunset, the face takes on a golden glow. Looking at the Eucharistic Lord for an hour transforms the heart in a mysterious way as the face of Moses was transformed after his companionship with God on the mountain. Something happens to us similar to that which happened to the disciples at Emmaus. On Easter Sunday afternoon when the Lord met them, he asked why they were so gloomy. After spending some time in his presence, and hearing again the secret of spirituality - 'The Son of Man must suffer to enter into his Glory'" - their time with him ended and their "hearts were on fire." — Bishop Fulton Sheen

How to Keep a Holy Hour

"I have found that it takes some time to catch fire in prayer. This has been one of the advantages of the daily Hour. It is not so brief as to prevent the soul from collecting itself and shaking off the multitudinous distractions of the world. Sitting before the Presence is like a body exposing itself before the sun to absorb its rays. Silence in the Hour is a tete-a-tete with the Lord. In those moments, one does not so much pour out written prayers, but listening takes its place. We do not say: 'Listen, Lord, for Thy servant speaks,' but 'Speak, Lord, for Thy servant heareth.'"— Bishop Fulton Sheen

"Know also that you will probably gain more by praying fifteen minutes before the Blessed Sacrament than by all the other spiritual exercises of the day. True, Our Lord hears our prayers anywhere, for He has made the promise, 'Ask, and you shall receive,' but He has revealed to His servants that those who visit Him in the Blessed Sacrament will obtain a more abundant measure of grace." — *St. Alphonsus Liguori*

Holy Hour Pages

"The purpose of the Holy Hour is to encourage deep personal encounter with Christ."

— *Bishop Fulton Sheen*

My Holy Hour

HOLY HOUR QUOTES

"When I am close to Jesus in the Blessed Sacrament, I feel as if my heart is bursting out of my chest."

—*St. Padre Pio*

"Prayer is the best weapon we possess. It is the key that opens the heart of God."

— *St. Padre Pio*

"Dear God, You generously blessed Your servant, St. Padre Pio, with the gifts of the Spirit. You marked his body with the five wounds of Christ Crucified, as a powerful witness to the saving Passion and Death of Your Son.

Endowed with the gift of discernment, St. Pio labored endlessly in the confessional for the salvation of souls. With reverence and intense devotion in the celebration of the Mass, he invited countless men and women to a greater union with Jesus Christ in the Sacrament of the Holy Eucharist.

Through the intercession of St. Padre Pio, I confidently beseech You to grant me the grace of (here state your petition).

— *Prayer for the Intercession of St. Padre Pio*

Record Your Favorite Quotes Here

REFLECTIONS

Personal Index

_____ *Pgs* ____

_____ *Pgs* ____

_____ *Pgs* ____

_____ *Pgs* ____

_____ *Pgs* ____

_____ *Pgs* ____

_____ *Pgs* ____

_____ *Pgs* ____

_____ *Pgs* ____

_____ *Pgs* ____

_____ *Pgs* ____

_____ *Pgs* ____

_____ *Pgs* ____

_____ *Pgs* ____

_____ *Pgs* ____

_____ *Pgs* ____

_____ *Pgs* ____

_____ *Pgs* ____

_____ *Pgs* ____

_____ *Pgs* ____

_____ *Pgs* ____

_____ *Pgs* ____

_____ *Pgs* ____

HOLY HOUR JOURNALS

Thank you for your interest in *Holy Hour Journals.* Discover more about using journals to deepen your prayer life by going to our website and getting a free copy of

How to Use a Prayer Journal during Holy Hour
www.HolyHourBooks.com

The Holy Hour Devotional Journal Series has been created to help Catholics from all walks of life to discover, explore, and enjoy the many rewards from a deeper connection to Christ.

Like our Facebook Page:
https://www.facebook.com/HolyHourBooks

Made in the USA
Monee, IL
21 December 2022

23280488R00076